Developing Literacy
TEXT LEVEL

TEXT-LEVEL ACTIVITIES FOR THE LITERACY HOUR

year

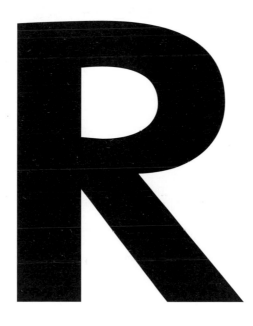

Ray Barker

Christine Moorcroft

A & C BLACK

Reprinted 2001
Published 2000 by
A&C Black (Publishers) Limited
37 Soho Square, London W1D 3QZ

ISBN 0-7136-5322-1

Acknowledgements
The authors and publishers are grateful for permission to reproduce the following:
page 32: *Elmer* © David McKee published by Andersen Press, London;
Thomas the Tank Engine © Britt Allcroft (Thomas) LLC,
published by Egmont Children's Books Limited and used with permission;
Rosie's Walk © Pat Hutchins, published by Bodley Head.

The authors and publishers would like to thank the following teachers
for their advice in producing this series of books:
Jane Beynon; Hardip Channa; Ann Hart; Lydia Hunt;
Rita Leader; Madeleine Madden; Helen Mason; Kim Pérez;
Joanne Turpin; Fleur Whatley

A CIP catalogue record for this book is
available from the British Library.

Printed in Great Britain by
St Edmundsbury Press Ltd, Bury St Edmunds, Suffolk.

Contents

Introduction

Developing Literacy: Text Level supports the teaching of reading and writing by providing a series of activities to develop children's ability to recognise and appreciate the different genres, styles and purposes of text. **Year R** encourages children to read text which they see around them in everyday life, as well as non-fiction and fiction books. It develops their enjoyment of rhymes and stories and provides frameworks which help them to compose their own. It also provides structures on which the children can base their non-fiction writing for particular purposes. The children learn about different kinds of text, including everyday text used in familiar situations (for example, road signs, menus and labels) as well as the words of rhymes and stories.

The activities are designed to be carried out in the time allocated to independent work during the Literacy Hour. They support the objectives of the National Literacy Strategy *Framework for Teaching* at text level and they incorporate strategies to encourage independent learning – for example, ways in which children can check their own work or that of a partner. For the younger children, it is assumed that an adult will read the instructions with them. Investigation is given greater emphasis as the series progresses towards **Year 6**.

Year R helps children to:

- understand print through shared reading and writing;
- recognise printed and handwritten words in different settings, and to distinguish between words and pictures;
- realise that words are written for many different purposes, and to write texts for different purposes, for example: sending messages, recording, informing and telling stories;
- appreciate that writing is written to be read again and always 'says the same thing';
- understand and use terms about books and print, for example: book, cover, title, beginning, end, page, word and letter;
- track text directionally, for example: from left to right and from page to page, and to understand that writing is formed letter by letter and word by word.

Year R also helps children to:

- read with understanding and to write;
- explore spoken and printed language;
- use cues which help them to read new words;
- appreciate the conventions of story-book language;
- re-tell familiar stories and to adapt them, for example, by changing their endings;
- experiment with, and adapt, rhymes;
- identify the order in which events happen in a story;
- identify significant parts of the text such as rhymes and repeated words;
- experiment with writing;
- write captions and labels and to write text to accompany pictures;
- plan their writing.

Extension

Most of the activity sheets end with a challenge (**Now try this!**) which reinforces and extends the children's learning and provides the teacher with an opportunity for assessment. These more challenging activities might be appropriate for only a few children; it is not expected that the whole class should complete them.

On some pages there is space for the children to complete the extension activities, but for others the children will require a notebook or separate sheet of paper.

Organisation

Few resources are needed besides scissors, glue, word-banks and simple dictionaries. Other materials are specified in the teachers' notes on the pages. Several activities are based on well-known fairy stories and nursery rhymes which the children need to have read, and to which they need access, but the activities have all been designed for use in conjuction with either readily available texts, or with texts of your choice.

To help teachers to select appropriate learning experiences for their pupils, the activities are grouped into sections within each book. The pages need not be presented in the order in which they appear in the books, unless otherwise stated.

Teachers' notes

Brief notes are provided at the bottom of most pages. They give ideas and suggestions for making the most of the activity sheet. They sometimes make suggestions for the whole class introduction, the plenary session or, possibly, for follow-up work using an adapted version of the activity sheet.

Structure of the Literacy Hour

The following chart shows an example of the way in which an activity from this book can be used to achieve the required organisation of the Literacy Hour.

Shopping (page 12)

Whole class introduction	15 min
Show the children carrier bags from familiar shops on which the names of the shops are written. Do they recognise any of them? Read the names of the shops, encouraging the children to join in. Read also any slogans on the bags.	

Whole class activity	15 min
Give selected children a card on which is written the name of a shop. Hold up a carrier bag and ask who has the name of the shop to which it belongs. The other children can read the name on the bag and check that the child who claims it is correct. When all the bags have been matched, pin them and the printed names on to a display board and read them with the children, pointing out any similarities and differences in the print.	

Group work	20 min	Independent work	20 min
In pairs, the children design and draw shops and carrier bags. One child in each pair draws a carrier bag for their shop, while the other draws the shop and writes its name on the bag. This could be combined with work in design technology, when they could make the carrier bags.		The others work independently from **Shopping** (page 12, **Developing Literacy: Text Level Year R**).	

Whole class plenary session	10 min
The children who have drawn shops and made carrier bags could hold them up for the others to read. They could stand in a semi-circle, holding their 'shops' (making a 'street' of shops), with their carrier bags mixed up on a table in front of them: the other children take turns to match a bag to a 'shop'.	

Using the activity sheets

Understanding of print: reading

Road signs (page 9) develops the children's ability to distinguish text (even if they cannot read it) from pictures. Before the activity, take the children out to look for and read road signs. On a recording sheet, they could tick those which they spot. During the Literacy Hour, use photographs of familiar road signs as shared texts. Which ones have the children seen before? Where? Do they know what they mean?

The kitchen cupboard (page 10) also develops the children's ability to distinguish text (even if they cannot read it) from pictures. Before the activity, read the labels of food containers with the children. The words might be difficult to read, but how can they tell what is in the containers? Encourage them to look carefully at the pictures.

Presents (page 11), **Shopping** (page 12) and **Class list** (page 13) develop the children's ability to recognise text and help them to understand that words can be written down to be read again. **Presents** and **Class list** can be linked to word-level work on names (see **Developing Literacy: Word Level Year R** and **Sentence Level Year R**).

Pet's passport (page 14) helps the children to recognise text and to learn about one of the contexts in which it is used (a form). Before the activity, read real passports (perhaps enlarged) and ask the children to point out the owner's photograph, name and other details. They could be given word-processed blank passport formats to complete for themselves and for pets.

In **Shopping list** (page 15) the children learn to recognise text and they find out about one of the contexts in which it is used. They learn that people write words in order to read them and that they write them for a purpose. The children could bring in shopping lists which their parents have written and used. Make a 'Shopping display' which includes shopping lists and other text connected with shopping: advertisements, labels, food containers, carrier bags and pictures of shop signs.

Book titles and covers (page 16) and **Pages** (page 17) help the children to learn and to use some of the terms connected with books: book, cover, title and page. Ask them to bring in their favourite books; they could point out the cover and title as well as other parts, such as the title page, the beginning, the ending and a line of text. **Pages** also develops the skill of tracking text from page to page.

Words and letters: 1 and **2** (pages 18–19) help the children to distinguish between words and letters and to use the terms 'word' and 'letter' correctly. Before this activity, write a selection of words and letters on individual cards and pin them to a board. Ask the children in turn to come out and remove 'a word' or 'a letter'. The game could be extended by adding cards on which a line of text is written.

Understanding of print: writing

Writing signs (page 20) is about one of the purposes of writing – to inform. The children decide what message they want to put on the park sign (for example 'No ball games (please)' or 'Please keep off the grass'. Some children might be able to make up a sign without using the words provided.

The pet shop (page 21) provides examples of print used in a familiar context. The children can work out from the pictures what kind of pet food is in each container and, if they cannot read the words in the word-bank, they can use the first phoneme to help them to select the correct word.

The car (page 22) and **The elephant** (page 23) highlight the difference between writing and drawings. Some children might need help in distinguishing the lines which link the words to the picture from the picture itself. They could first label a picture by linking words written on cards to the picture by means of coloured threads.

Making words (page 24) focuses on the distinction between letters and words and reinforces the children's understanding that words are made up of letters. The children could practise making up words from a limited number of plastic or wooden letters.

Teddy's birthday (page 25) provides practice in writing for an everyday purpose; the children practise writing their names as well as familiar greetings.

Going home (page 26) consolidates the children's understanding of the conventional left-to-right direction of text in English. Children whose home language is written from right to left (for example, Arabic) might need extra practice in this. They could demonstrate this difference for others in the class, perhaps by showing greetings cards (see page 31).

A menu (page 27) is an example of text used for an everyday purpose; it provides pictures and text to help the children plan their own menu using **Make a menu** (page 28). It can be linked with role-play in a class 'restaurant' or 'café'. Some children might be able to plan their menus using information from illustrated menus from restaurants.

The catalogue: toys and **The catalogue: order form** (pages 29–30) are also examples of text used in an everyday context. They could be linked with role-play in a class 'toy shop', in which real catalogues and order forms are provided.

Reading comprehension

Cards (page 31) is designed to encourage the children to use cues when reading: here, the pictures on the cards help them to read the words. This activity can be linked with work in religious education on celebrations during which the children can investigate other greetings cards.

Animal stories (page 32), like **Cards**, encourages the children to use cues when reading (the pictures on the book covers); it can also be used to introduce vocabulary about books ('cover' and 'title'). The activity introduces summary and prediction at a very simple level ('What is the book about?' or 'What do you think the book is going to be about?').

Story book cover (page 33) extends and consolidates the children's vocabulary about books ('title' and 'cover'). Other vocabulary about books can be introduced: 'back cover', 'title page', 'author' and 'illustrator'.

Story book and character cards (pages 34–35) use the word 'character' for a person or animal in a story (see also page 26). The children could paint pictures of the characters in the stories which have been read with the class. Make the books available for the children to read before and during the activity.

Molly's walk (page 36) develops the children's recognition of repetitive language in a story. It is based on *We're Going on a Bear Hunt* (Michael Rosen, Walker) which can be read first; afterwards, ask the children to identify each problem faced by the family in the story and how the family overcame it.

Story mix-up (pages 37–38) encourages the children to re-read familiar stories. The activities also develop their recognition of characters and plots of familiar stories. During the week before the children attempt the activity sheets, read to or with them *Little Red Riding Hood* and *Cinderella*. Make these books available for them to look at during the activity.

Who says this? (page 39) helps the children to recognise significant parts of a text, such as speech that is repeated by a story character. During the reading of shared texts, they can join in these repeated words, which can also be displayed (in speech bubbles) alongside pictures of the characters.

Beginnings (page 40) develops the children's understanding of story book language and how it is used, by introducing some of the formal elements of traditional stories. A display can be made of 'story language', which the children can look for in the stories they read (and use in the stories they write). Modern story books which begin with 'Once' include: *Can't You Sleep, Little Bear?* (Martin Waddell, Walker) and *Bye Bye Baby* (Janet & Allan Ahlberg, Mammoth); others which begin 'There was once…' include *Once There Were Giants* (Martin Waddell, Walker) and *Elmer* (David McKee, Andersen Press). Examples of books which begin with a statement about time are *The Tiny Seed* ('It is autumn…') and *The Bad-Tempered Ladybird* ('It was night…') (both by Eric Carle, Puffin).

Nursery rhyme pairs (pages 41–42) is about well-known rhymes, which should be read with the children during the week or so before they attempt the activity. This activity could be used to assess the children's learning at the end of a topic on nursery rhymes.

In **Incey Wincey Spider** (page 43) the children re-read a well-known rhyme and match the words to the pictures. Few of them will be able to read all the words of the rhyme, but they should be encouraged to use cues such as the initial phonemes of words and recognition of high-frequency words (such as 'all', 'and', 'the', 'up').

Wrong rhyme (page 44) encourages the children to read carefully and develops their awareness of the need for text to make sense. It can be read aloud with them to encourage them to match the spoken words with the printed ones.

Action rhyme (pages 45–46) encourages the children to use pictorial cues when reading. They learn some useful words by matching them with pictures and by taking part in the action rhyme. They need to have practised the rhyme as a class several times before attempting the activity.

Finding out about eggs (page 47) and **Toys** (page 48) are about reading information books. The children are encouraged to use both pictures and text to find information and then to write, in a different form, what they have found out. Both activities can be linked with work in science, on animals and sound respectively.

Writing composition

Finger puppets (page 49) encourages the children to experiment with role-play; it provides characters which the children can use to tell a story to a friend. They can speak as if they are the character itself as they work the finger puppet. The term 'character' is consolidated and the children could name the characters in stories they know.

Teddy bears' picnic (page 50) helps the children to use their experience of familiar stories and rhymes to begin to write a story. Before the activity, they could have a real teddy bears' picnic to which they bring their teddy bears, or the activity could be used after the Literacy Hour to plan such an event. For the extension activity, some children might only be able to label the things they have drawn; others could tell a story about the scene, and some might be able to write a story.

Story map (page 51) provides the setting and direction for a story. Drawing on their experiences of fairy tales and modern stories, the children can make up events which happen as their character passes each place on the pictorial map. A large version of the story map can be made to fit a display board, and the children's stories can be fixed next to the places in which they happened.

Story starters (page 52) helps the children to plan a story in terms of the beginning, the middle and the ending. It provides twelve cards depicting scenes in which a story can take place. The children can choose a card and talk about what might happen in the setting, what might be hiding in it or what they might discover if they go into one of the places such as the hollow tree or the cave.

Story cards (page 53) helps the children to plan a story in terms of the beginning, the middle and the ending. Each card gives the setting of a story followed by a picture to suggest what might happen there. They can make up the ending of the story and can tell the story to a partner.

A different ending (page 54) also helps the children to plan a story in terms of the beginning, the middle and the ending. It depicts the beginning and middle of a well-known story *(The Gingerbread Man)*, with two new endings. The children can tell the story, elaborating on the text provided and choosing one of the endings. Some children might be able to think up another ending, which they could draw and perhaps write.

Story character (page 55) encourages the children to experiment with writing stories. It presents a strange-looking character about which they can invent a story. They begin by talking about and drawing a room in the home of the character. Ask them what might be in the room ('What kind of chairs, if any, might there be?' 'Would the creature sit on chairs, or on something else? What?' 'Would there be a carpet? What would it be like? If not, what might be on the floor?').

What might happen here? (page 56) encourages the children to use their experience of fairy stories to make up a story which could happen in a castle. They complete the picture and talk to a partner about what is happening in it before writing the story.

Biscuits (page 57) is a non-fiction chronological text. It provides the children with an opportunity to write sentences about pictures, having described what is taking place.

The cook's shopping list (page 58) is based on the children's experience of everyday non-fiction texts – shopping lists. They can make use of their knowledge of the format of a shopping list by writing the items in a column.

Memory board (page 59) is based on the children's experience of everyday non-fiction texts – messages on memory boards. A class memory board could be provided on to which the children can pin their own messages.

Boat race (page 60) develops the children's skills in writing accounts of what they have done and found out during work in other subjects, such as science. It encourages them to look at pictures as well as text in order to find information. The picture provides them with all the information they need, and all the words they need are in the word-bank.

A letter to Humpty Dumpty (page 61) develops the children's awareness of, and skills in, writing in order to communicate; here they write to a well-known character, using a verse to provide a context for the letter. A 'reply from Humpty Dumpty' could be written by the teacher, displayed in the classroom and read with the children; this could lead to a series of letters between the children and Humpty Dumpty. The use of a question to invite a reply is a feature of letter-writing which the children need to learn.

Rhyme change (page 62) requires the children to explore rhymes; they begin with a well-known rhyme which is changed to encourage them to play with rhyming words. To help them, a 'rhyming word-bank' could be made with the children during the introductory session.

Zoo poem (page 63) is about exploring sounds. The children write the sounds made by the animals. This is also an opportunity for the teacher to assess the children's ability to use what they have learned about spelling and phonics – the children can spell the animal sounds phonetically.

Musical poem (page 64), like **Zoo poem**, is about exploring sounds. The children write the sounds made by the instruments. This activity prepares the children for later work on onomatopoeia as they say and then write the sounds of the instruments.

Glossary of terms used

fairy tale A story which includes element of magic and magical folk, such as fairies, elves and goblins.

genre A specific type of writing or other medium of communication, for example: legend, newspaper story or poem.

onomatopoeia The use of words which echo sounds associated with their meaning, for example: *bang, boom, squeak*.

pronoun A word used instead of a noun, for example: (personal pronouns) *I, you, he, she, it, we, they*; (dependent possessive pronouns) *my, your, her, his, its, our, their*; (independent possessive pronouns) *mine, yours, his, hers, its, ours, theirs*.

recount A text (or part of a text) written to re-tell for information or entertainment. It uses descriptive language, might include dialogue and is usually written in the past tense.

report A non-chronological text, usually written in the present tense, that describes or classifies.

rime The part of a syllable which contains the vowel and final consonant or consonant cluster, if there is one, for example: <u>c</u>at, <u>c</u>ow.

title The name of a book, play, poem, etc, but also part of a person's name: for example, *Mr, Mrs, Miss* and *Ms*. A person's title always begins with a capital letter. *Mr* and *Mrs* are abbreviations of *Mister* and *Mistress* (which has become corrupted to *Missus* or *Missis*). *Ms* is a modern abbreviation of a woman's title (*Mrs* and/or *Miss*), by analogy with *Mr*.

- **Tick the signs with writing on them.**

 ☐

 ☐

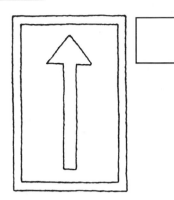 ☐

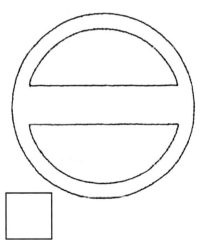 ☐

 ☐

 ☐

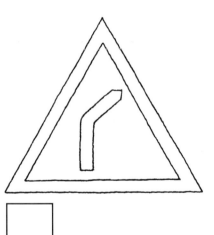 ☐

 ☐

 ☐

- **Draw another sign with writing on it.**
- **Draw another sign with no writing.**

Teachers' note You could provide cut-out pictures of road signs for the children to sort into two sets: those with writing on them and those without. For the extension activity, a copy of *The Highway Code* would be useful.

**Developing Literacy
Text Level Year R
© A & C Black 2000**

The kitchen cupboard

- **Colour the things with writing on them.**

Now try this!

- **Find another food package.**
- **Draw a picture of it.**
- **Copy the writing on it.**

Teachers' note To introduce this activity, you could read the names on labels of food packages with the children and, for a group activity, provide cards on which the names of foods are written for the children to match with the packages themselves.

Developing Literacy
Text Level Year R
© A & C Black 2000

Presents

• **Write the children's names on their presents.**

• **Write your friends' names on these presents.**

Now try this!

Teachers' note Before the activity, ensure that there are several places in the classroom where the names of the children are written. Hold up cards bearing the names of children in the class: can the others read them? Can they see the same name written anywhere else?

Developing Literacy
Text Level Year R
© A & C Black 2000

11

Shopping

- **Match the carrier bags to the shops.**

- **Draw carrier bags for these shops.**

Now try this!

SWEETIE

FISH AND CHIPS

Teachers' note To introduce the activity, you could show the children carrier bags from familiar shops, and ask them which shops the bags come from. (For safety, the bags can be cut in two.) During a group activity, the children could match the handwritten names of shops with the carrier bags.

Developing Literacy
Text Level Year R
© A & C Black 2000

Class list

• **Join the children to their names.**

Tom Adams
Sara Catt
Carl Dunn
Rosie Fine
Helen Low
Mariam Musa

 • **Draw three children in your group.**

• **Write their names.**

Teachers' note The children could also match handwritten names on cards with the same names printed in different fonts.

Developing Literacy
Text Level Year R
© A & C Black 2000

Pet's passport

• Read the passport.

Passport

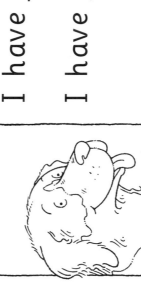

Name Fido

Animal dog

Eyes brown

Hair brown and white

Ears long

• Fill in the gaps.

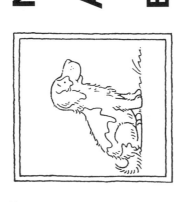

My name is _____ .

I am a _____ .

I have _____ eyes.

I have _____ hair.

I have _____ ears.

Word-bank

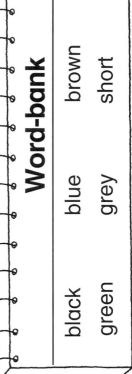

black	blue	brown	ginger
green	grey	short	white

• Make a passport for a cat.

Now try this!

Teachers' note In the extension activity, some children might be able to add the cat's date of birth and other details, such as its size. Point out that the children themselves choose the cat's name and decide what colour eyes and hair to give it.

Developing Literacy
Text Level Year R
© A & C Black 2000

Shopping list

- **Read Lisa's shopping list.**
- **Look at what she has bought.**
- **Tick the words on the list.** ✓

apples
biscuits ✓
butter
cabbage
cheese
crisps
jam
lemonade
milk
pasta
pizza
rice
soup
yogurt

rice
milk
lemonade
crisps
pasta
soup
butter
cheese
pizza
biscuits

Now try this!

- **Draw three other things for Lisa's shopping list.**
- **Write the words.**

Teachers' note You could introduce the activity with a display-sized shopping list (laminated for re-use and illustrated with food packages and pictures from magazines to act as cues for reading). Ask the children to examine a basket of shopping and to tick the things on the list which have been bought.

Developing Literacy
Text Level Year R
© A & C Black 2000

Book titles and covers

• **Match the titles to the covers.**

Flowers

Horses

Castles

Snails

Birds

Trees

Cars

Planes

Now try this!

• **Draw a cover for a book about butterflies.**

• **Write the title.**

Teachers' note Introduce the activity by covering the titles of books. Ask the children what the books are about and what they think the title might be. How can they tell? The children could match the titles (written on cards) to the books.

Developing Literacy
Text Level Year R
© A & C Black 2000

Pages

Here are some pages from a book.

- **Cut out the pages.**
- **Put them in order.**
- **Read the book.**

There were
four chicks.

The eggs
cracked.

Four little heads
came out.

The hen laid
four eggs.

- **Make a cover for the book.**
- **Write a title.**

Teachers' note In the extension activity, the children could also make a title page for the book, number the pages and staple them together in the right order. Old, tattered story books could be taken apart for the children to put in order.

Developing Literacy
Text Level Year R
© A & C Black 2000

Words and letters: 1

- **Colour red the shapes with a** $\boxed{\text{word}}$.

- **Colour blue the shapes with a** $\boxed{\text{letter}}$.

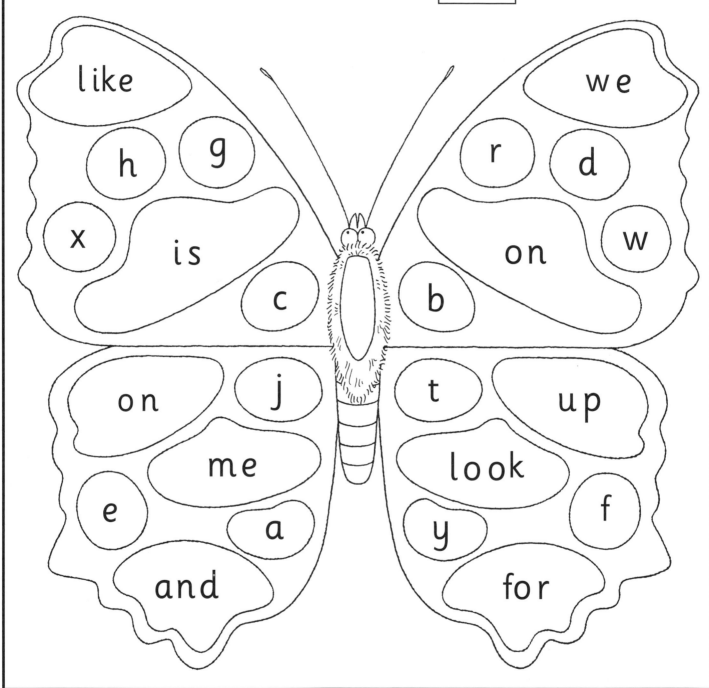

- **Draw another butterfly with words and letters on it.**

- **Read the words to a partner.**

Teachers' note For the extension activity, the butterfly on this page could be copied with the letters and words masked. For further practice, other copies could be made with different letters and different high-frequency words.

Developing Literacy
Text Level Year R
© A & C Black 2000

18

Words and letters: 2

- **Colour green the shapes with a word .**
- **Colour yellow the shapes with a letter .**

- **Write all the words you found.**
- **Read the words to a partner.**
- **Draw your own picture with words and letters.**

Now try this!

Teachers' note For the extension activity, the scene on this page could be copied with the letters and words masked. For further practice, other copies could be made with different letters and different high-frequency words.

Developing Literacy
Text Level Year R
© A & C Black 2000

• **Write a message on the sign.**

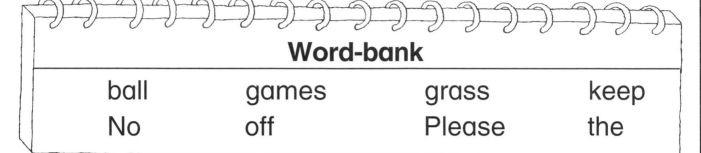

Word-bank

ball	games	grass	keep
No	off	Please	the

Now try this!

• **Make a sign for your classroom.**

Teachers' note Before the activity, encourage the children to notice signs they see when they are out and about. Pictures of such signs (in context) could be read as shared texts: for example, 'Open', 'Closed', 'No parking'. Do the children recognise the signs?

Developing Literacy
Text Level Year R
© A & C Black 2000

The pet shop

• **Write the labels on the pet foods.**

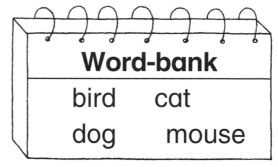

Word-bank

bird   cat

dog   mouse

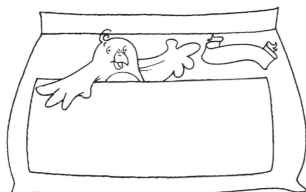

Now try this!

• **Draw a packet of hamster food.**

• **Write the label.**

Teachers' note As shared texts, you could read the labels and packets of pet foods (if necessary photocopy and enlarge them). Ask the children what kind of animal eats each food: how can they tell? (If necessary, point out the pictures.)

Developing Literacy
Text Level Year R
© A & C Black 2000

The car

- **Join the words to the parts of the car.**

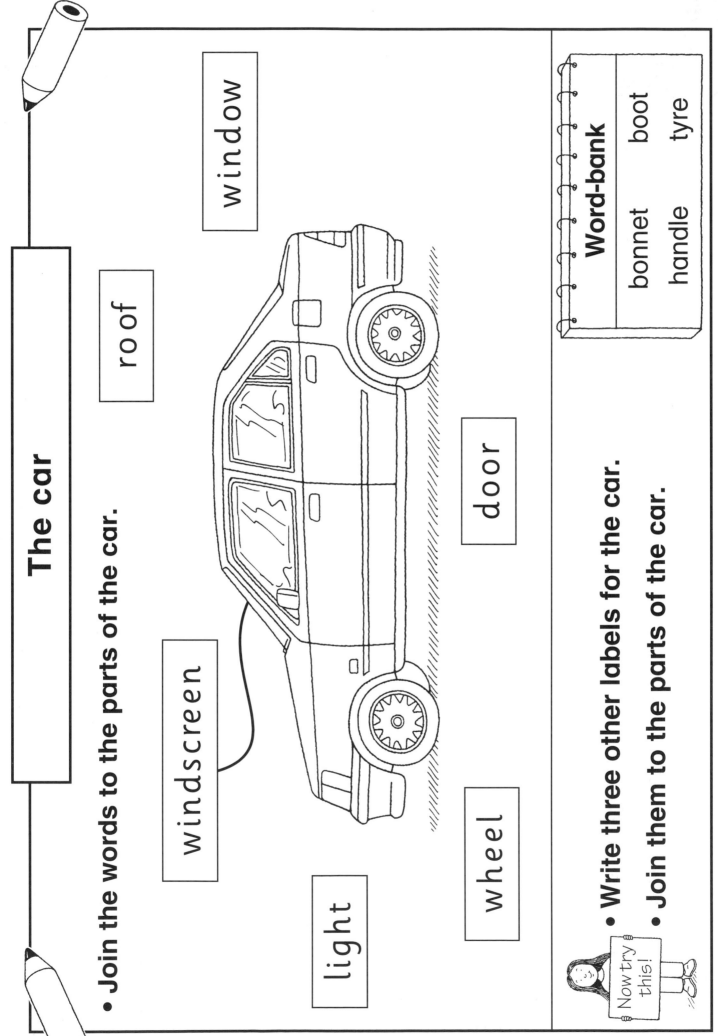

window

roof

windscreen

light

wheel

door

Word-bank

bonnet   boot

handle   tyre

Now try this!

- **Write three other labels for the car.**
- **Join them to the parts of the car.**

Teachers' note To introduce the activity, you could show the children a toy car and ask them to name the parts of it; write the names of the parts on cards and link them to the parts of the car with wool or string. Mix up the labels and ask the children to sort them out.

Developing Literacy
Text Level Year R

The elephant

- Write labels for the elephant.
- Join them to the parts of the elephant.

Word-bank

ear
eye
leg
tail
trunk
tusk

Use information books.

- Draw and label another animal.

Now try this!

Teachers' note To introduce the activity you might like to display a large picture of an elephant (you could enlarge this one) and ask the children to name the parts of it. Write the names of the parts on cards, fix them around the picture and draw lines to link them to the parts of the elephant. Mix up the labels and ask the children to sort them out.

Developing Literacy
Text Level Year R
© A & C Black 2000

Making words

- **Cut out the letters.**

a	a	b	c
e	e	g	l
m	n	t	t

- **Use the letters to make these words.**

b a t		l e g		c a t		m e n

- **Use the letters to make six other words.**
- **Write the words.**

Teachers' note You could laminate the sheet before cutting out the letter cards, so that they can be re-used. To introduce the activity, write some three-letter words on the board. Invite the children to copy the words using plastic or wooden letters which can be fixed to the display board.

Developing Literacy
Text Level Year R
© A & C Black 2000

Teddy's birthday

- ## Write the label.

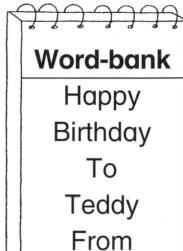

To _____

From

_____

Word-bank

Happy
Birthday
To
Teddy
From

- ## Make a birthday card for Teddy.

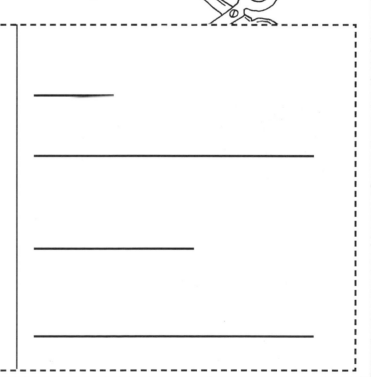

 - ## Make a birthday card for someone you know.

Now try this!

Teachers' note You could read birthday cards (perhaps the children's own cards) as shared texts, then ask the children about the words which are often seen on birthday cards. Write the words on the board. In the second part of the activity, when the children have cut out and folded the card, help them to work out on which side they should draw a picture.

Developing Literacy
Text Level Year R
© A & C Black 2000

Going home

- **Trace the arrows.**
- **Complete the sentences.**

Word-bank

boy   dog
horse   mouse

 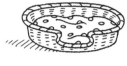

The cat goes home.

The ___ goes home.

___ ____ goes home.

____ ___ ____ home.

___ ____ ___ ____ .

 • **Draw and write about another animal going home.**

Now try this!

Teachers' note Model the completed example with the children: they should follow the arrow with their finger while reading the sentence. In their reading, encourage them to use cues such as the picture and the first phoneme of the word in the word-bank.

**Developing Literacy
Text Level Year R
© A & C Black 2000**

A menu

- **Choose one thing from each part of the menu.** ☑

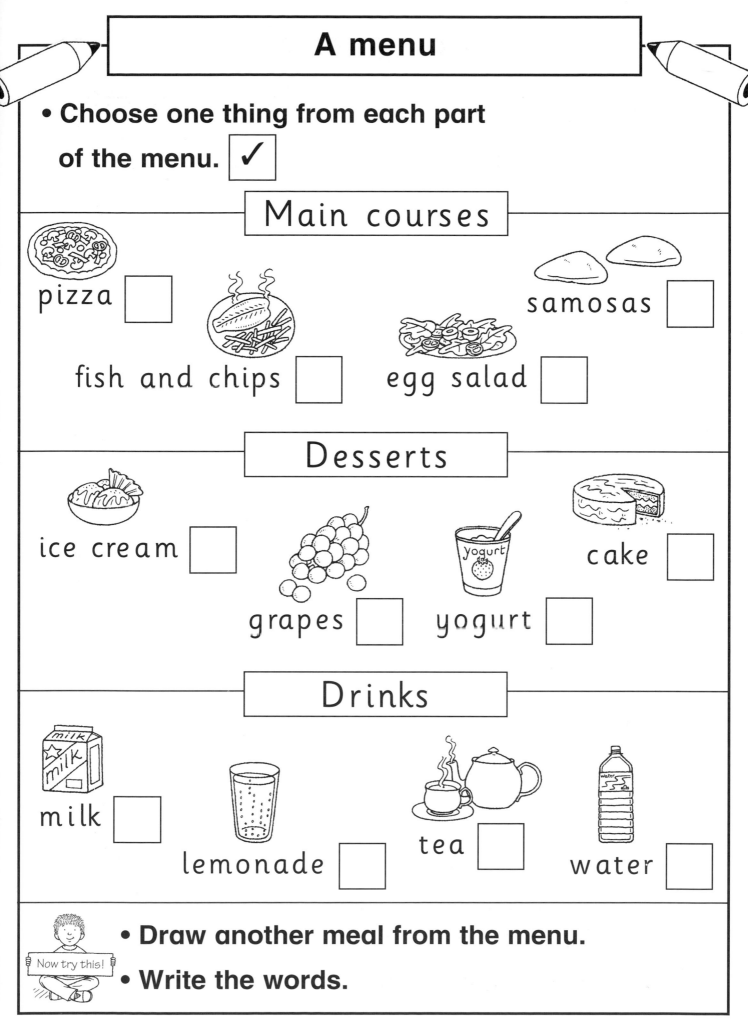

Main courses

pizza ☐

fish and chips ☐

egg salad ☐

samosas ☐

Desserts

ice cream ☐

grapes ☐

yogurt ☐

cake ☐

Drinks

milk ☐

lemonade ☐

tea ☐

water ☐

Now try this!

- **Draw another meal from the menu.**
- **Write the words.**

Teachers' note Use this with page 28. Before the activity, to familiarise the children with the language of menus, you could collect and display illustrated menus which can be read with groups of children.

Developing Literacy
Text Level Year R
© A & C Black 2000

- **Draw three things in each part of the menu.**
- **Write the words.**

Write your café's name at the top of the menu.

Main courses

Desserts

Drinks

Teachers' note The children should first complete page 27. Before the activity, to familiarise the children with the language of menus, you could collect and display illustrated menus to read with groups of children. Some children might be able to make their own menu formats, perhaps including starters as well as the other courses.

Developing Literacy
Text Level Year R
© A & C Black 2000

The catalogue: toys

- **Match the words to the pictures.**

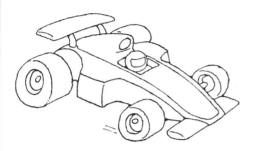  

| doll's pram £19.99 | painting set £8.50 | computer game £12.99 |

| racing car £4.99 | doll's house £29.99 | swing £49.50 |

  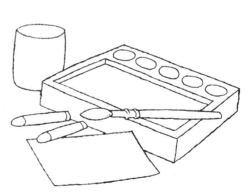

- **Draw two other toys.**
- **Write the words.**

Developing Literacy
Text Level Year R
© A & C Black 2000

The catalogue: order form

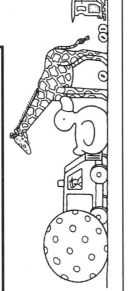

- Choose two toys from a catalogue.
- Fill in this order form.

Name		Date	
Number	Toy		Price

- Write your address on the label.

Now try this!

Address

Teachers' note Use this with page 29. Give the children real catalogues and encourage them to copy the code for each toy from the catalogue page. You could read an enlarged mail order catalogue page as a shared text in which the

Developing Literacy
Text Level Year R

30

Cards

- ## Join the pictures to the cards.

- ## Draw another kind of card.

Teachers' note Encourage the children to bring in used greetings cards of different types
which they can read to the rest of the class, saying to whom the cards were sent and why.

Developing Literacy
Text Level Year R
© A & C Black 2000

Animal stories

• **Tick the books about animals.** ✓

The Big Pancake

Jack and the Beanstalk

Elmer

Puss in Boots

Thomas the Tank Engine

Goldilocks and the Three Bears

The Three Little Pigs

The Gingerbread Man

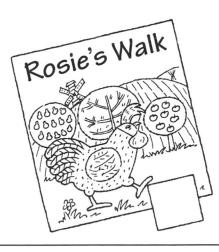

Rosie's Walk

Now try this!

• **Find two other books about animals.**

• **Draw the covers.**

• **Write the titles.**

Teachers' note You might like to introduce the activity by holding up books which the children know, and asking if they are about an animal, and what *kind* of animal. Do the same with books the children do not know; ask them how they can tell, from the cover picture, what a book will be about.

Developing Literacy
Text Level Year R
© A & C Black 2000

32

Story book cover

• **Write the title on this book cover.**

Now try this!

• **Draw the cover of your favourite story book.**
• **Write the title.**
• **Write the author's name.**

Teachers' note Before the children attempt this activity they need to be familiar with traditional tales such as *Rapunzel* (depicted here). Provide a copy of the book. Discuss what is on the covers of books of this kind – the title and a picture. The children could also look at book covers which show the author's name.

Developing Literacy
Text Level Year R
© A & C Black 2000

Story book cards

Cinderella

The Three Billy Goats Gruff

Little Red Riding Hood

The Frog Prince

Snow White and the Seven Dwarfs

Hansel and Gretel

Sleeping Beauty

Jack and the Beanstalk

The Gingerbread Man

Teachers' note You might want to photocopy the page on to card and laminate it for re-use before cutting out the story book cards. Show the children the books to which they refer and ask them which of the stories they know. (Continued on page 35.)

Developing Literacy
Text Level Year R
© A & C Black 2000

Character cards

Ugly sisters

The troll

The wolf

The frog

The wicked queen

The witch

The good fairy

The giant

The fox

Teachers' note (Continued from page 34.) You might want to photocopy the page on to card and laminate it for re-use before cutting out the character cards. In groups, the children match the characters to the books or play 'matching pairs' (with the cards on page 34) by taking turns to turn over two cards: if they match, they keep them, if not they replace them.

Developing Literacy
Text Level Year R
© A & C Black 2000

Molly's walk

- **Read the story.**

- **Write the missing words.**

Molly is going for a walk.

Oh, no! A wall!
I can't go round it!
I can't go under it!
I'll have to go over it!

Oh, no! A stream!
I can't go round it!
I can't go under it!
I'll have to go over it!

_____!   Mud!

I can't go _____!

I can't go _____!

I'll have to go _____!

Now try this!

- **Draw another picture for the story.**

- **Write the words.**

Teachers' note Read the story with the children, encouraging them to join in. They could also invent new obstacles which Molly encounters on her walk, and make up words (following the repetitive pattern) to say how she gets past the obstacles. The children could cut up the pictures and use them to make a story book.

36

Developing Literacy
Text Level Year R
© A & C Black 2000

- **Cut out the covers and the pages.**
- **Put the two stories in the right order.**
- **Put the correct cover on top.**

Cinderella

Little Red Riding Hood

The woodcutter comes.

A fairy helps Cinderella.

Now try this!

Work with a partner.

- **Choose one of the stories.**
- **Draw the next picture.**
- **Write the words.**

Teachers' note Ensure that the children are familiar with both stories before they attempt this activity. Cut off and retain the extension activity and let the children cut out and sort the story sections, which they could read with a partner. (Continued on page 38.)

Developing Literacy
Text Level Year R
© A & C Black 2000

She has to go home
at midnight.

Red Riding Hood goes
to see Grandma.

The wolf eats
Red Riding Hood.

Cinderella wants to
go to the ball.

Cinderella dances
with the prince.

Grandma looks like a
wolf. It is the wolf!

Teachers' note (Continued from page 37.) When the children have completed the extension activity, they could staple one set of pages together in book form, adding the page they have made.

Developing Literacy
Text Level Year R
© A & C Black 2000

Who says this?

- **Read the words.**

- **Match them to the characters.**

> Fee, fi, fo, fum, I smell the blood of a little man!

> Run, run, as fast as you can — You can't catch me, I'm the gingerbread man.

> I'm a troll fol de rol!

> I'll huff and I'll puff, and I'll blow your house down.

- **Who says this?**

> Who's been sitting in my chair?

- **Draw the character.**

Teachers' note The children should work on this activity in pairs. Before they begin, provide copies of the books for the children to read, and read the stories to or with the children.

Developing Literacy
Text Level Year R
© A & C Black 2000

Beginnings

- **Find stories which begin with** Once .
- **Fill in the chart.**

Story	Beginning
The Magic Porridge Pot	Once upon a time

- **Write another way to begin a story.**

Now try this!

Developing Literacy
Text Level Year R
© A & C Black 2000

Teachers' note You could discuss the beginnings of traditional stories, and show examples of some modern stories which also begin with 'Once'. For the extension activity, provide stories with different beginnings which follow a pattern (such as a statement about the time, season or weather).

Nursery rhyme pairs: 1

Little Bo Peep

sheep

Little Miss Muffet

a great spider

the Queen of Hearts

tarts

Mary

a little lamb

Little Boy Blue

Teachers' note You might want to photocopy the page on to card and laminate it for re-use before attempting this activity, the children need to be familiar with the nursery rhymes represented. Encourage them to say the rhymes to help them to pair the cards. (Continued on page 42.)

Developing Literacy
Text Level Year R
© A & C Black 2000

Nursery rhyme pairs: 2

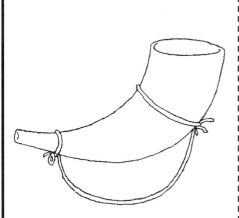a horn	three blind mice	the farmer's wife
the little nut tree	a silver nutmeg and a golden pear	Simple Simon
a pieman	Incey Wincey Spider	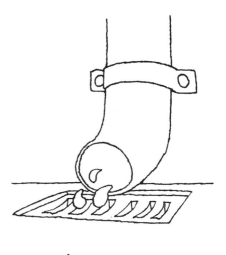the spout

Teachers' note (Continued from page 41.) You might want to photocopy the page on to card and laminate it for re-use before cutting out the cards. Groups of children could match the cards or play 'matching pairs' by taking turns to turn over two cards: if they match, they keep them, if not they replace them.

Developing Literacy
Text Level Year R
© A & C Black 2000

Incey Wincey Spider

- **Put the pictures in the right order.**

- **Match the words to the pictures.**

One picture is missing.

- **Read the rhyme.**

| Incey Wincey Spider climbed up the spout again. | Out came the sun and dried up all the rain; |
| Down came the rain and washed the spider out; | Incey Wincey Spider climbed up the spout; |

- **Draw the missing picture.**

Now try this!

Teachers' note Repeat the rhyme with the children several times before they attempt the activity, and encourage them to say it aloud to help them to put the pictures in order.

Developing Literacy
Text Level Year R
© A & C Black 2000

Wrong rhyme

- **Read the rhyme.**

- **Ring the words which are wrong.**

Humpty Dumpty sat on a well.

Humpty Dumpty had a great fire.

All the king's hats
And at the king's men,

Couldn't pat Humpty together again.

- **Write the rhyme correctly.**

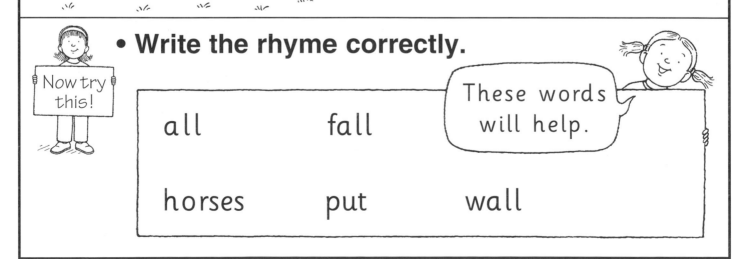

Now try this!

These words will help.

all	fall	
horses	put	wall

Teachers' note To introduce the activity, you could read an enlarged copy of the (correct version) of the rhyme with the children. Have one child point to each word as it is read. During the plenary session, the children could report the changes they have made to the rhyme on this page.

Developing Literacy
Text Level Year R
© A & C Black 2000

Action rhyme: 1

- **Look at the pictures.**
- **Read the words.**

Do the actions!

 head	 shoulders	 knees
 toes	 eyes	 ears
 mouth	 nose	Now try this! • **Read the words aloud.** • **Ask a partner to do the actions!**

Teachers' note Write the rhyme *Head, shoulders, knees and toes* (on page 46) on the board and display large copies of the pictures. Read it, pointing to the pictures, with the children joining in and doing the actions. In the extension activity the children can check what their partner does against the pictures. (Continued on page 46.)

Developing Literacy
Text Level Year R
© A & C Black 2000

Action rhyme: 2

• **Complete the rhyme.**

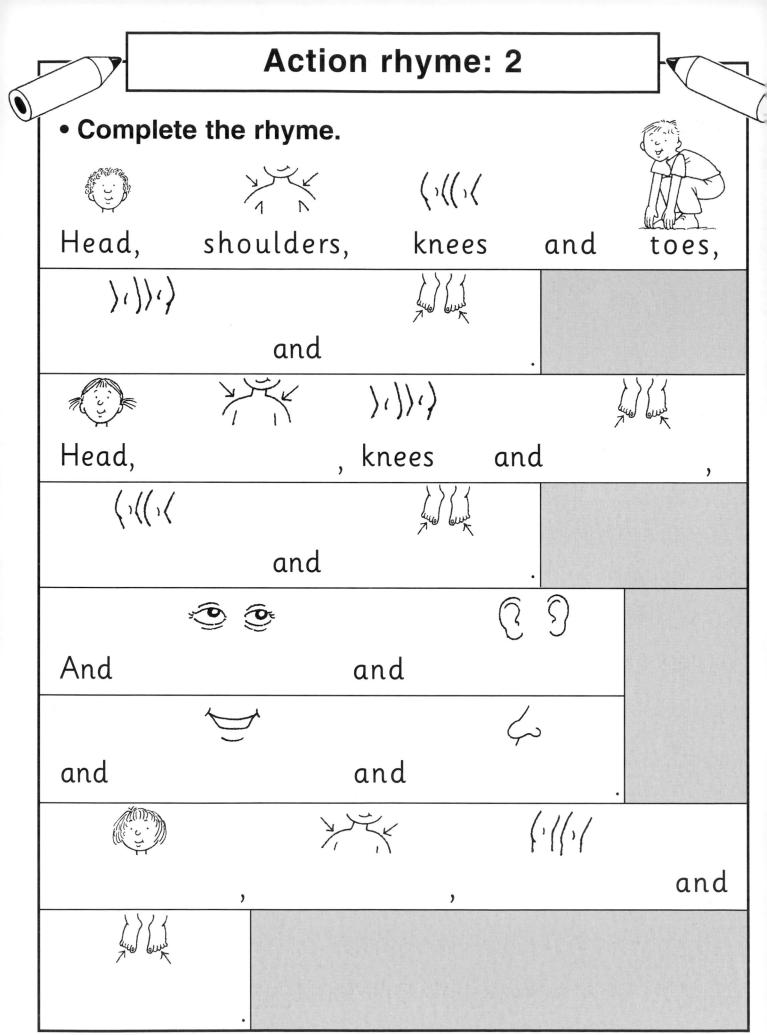

Head,   shoulders,   knees   and   toes,

and

.

Head,   , knees   and   ,

and

.

And   and

and   and   .

,   ,   and

.

Teachers' note The children will need to refer to a copy of page 45. During the plenary session the children could take turns to read out a line of the verse, while the others listen and check it. This activity could be linked with work in science on 'Ourselves'.

Developing Literacy
Text Level Year R
© A & C Black 2000

Finding out about eggs

• **Read the words and look at the pictures.**

Animals which lay eggs

Hens lay eggs.

Snails lay eggs.

Worms lay eggs.

Spiders lay eggs.

Ants lay eggs.

Crocodiles lay eggs.

What have you found out?

• **Tick the animals which lay eggs.** ✓

ant		lion		
cat		rabbit		
crocodile		snail		
dog		spider		
hen		worm		

Now try this!

• **Find out about another animal which lays eggs.**

Read information books.

Teachers' note Read the text with the children while they point to each word in turn, encouraging them to use the pictures as cues in their reading. In the extension activity they could contribute to a class wallchart about animals which lay eggs.

Developing Literacy
Text Level Year R
© A & C Black 2000

Toys

- **Look at the pictures.**

- **Read the words.**

 drum	 paints	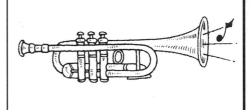 trumpet
 blocks	 whistle	 police car

- **Fill in the chart.**

Noisy toys	Quiet toys

 Now try this!

- **Write some other toys on the chart.**

Teachers' note The children could use a similar chart to record information they have found about other topics, for example: 'animals' and 'plants' or 'living' and 'not living'.

Developing Literacy
Text Level Year R
© A & C Black 2000

Finger puppets

• **Use the finger puppets to tell a story.**

Now try this!

• **Draw pictures of your story.**
• **Write your story.**

Teachers' note Cut out the puppets and the finger holes before giving them to the children with
the bottom part of the sheet. You could introduce the activity by putting puppets on the fingers of
each hand and telling a story (or adapt a well-known story), with the puppets carrying out the actions
and saying the words. Make a word-bank of story vocabulary in response to the children's ideas.

Developing Literacy
Text Level Year R
© A & C Black 2000

Teddy bears' picnic

- **Draw the picnic.**
- **Write the words.**

Word-bank

apple	bun
cake	drink
samosa	sandwich

- **Write about the picnic.**

Now try this!

Teachers' note You could read stories and information books about picnics with the children and ask them what kinds of foods they like to have on picnics. What do they think their teddy bears would like? You could adapt or extend the word-bank to incorporate the children's ideas.

Developing Literacy
Text Level Year R
© A & C Black 2000

50

Story map

- **Move a character along the path.**
- **Tell the story to a partner.**

You need

a small model person

start

finish

Now try this!

- **Draw something which happened in your story.**
- **Write about it.**

Teachers' note You could introduce story maps by making a large pictorial map and 'walking' a cardboard character around it, asking the children what the character can see, feel and hear. What does the character do? What problems does the character face and how does he or she overcome them?

Developing Literacy
Text Level Year R
© A & C Black 2000

Story starters

Teachers' note You might want to photocopy the page on to card and laminate it for re-use before cutting out the cards. The children choose a 'Story starter' card from which to begin a story. They could tell a partner what else is in the picture which cannot be seen, who might be hidden there and what they might be doing.

Developing Literacy
Text Level Year R
© A & C Black 2000

Story cards

Teachers' note This page could be laminated for re-use. Cut out the cards. Ask the children to choose one of them and tell the story to a partner, making up the ending. In a guided writing session the children could tell their story to a group. Some children might be able to write their stories.

Developing Literacy
Text Level Year R
© A & C Black 2000

A different ending

- **Choose an ending for the story.**
- **Tell the story to a friend.**

Ending

Follow that bus!

Middle

The gingerbread man ran away.

Beginning

An old woman made a gingerbread man.

- **Draw another ending.**

Now try this!

Teachers' note You may wish to read with the children the story of *The Gingerbread Man* before they tackle this activity.

Developing Literacy
Text Level Year R
© A & C Black 2000

Story character

- Give the story character a name.

- Draw a room for him or her.

- Tell a partner what the character does there.

- Write about what happens to the character in the room.

Teachers' note Discuss the character shown on the page; is this a real person? How can the children tell? Ask them in what sort of home they think the character lives. Make a word-bank of vocabulary in response to their ideas, for the children to use in their stories.

Developing Literacy
Text Level Year R
© A & C Black 2000

What might happen here?

- **Finish the picture to show** what might happen here.
- **Draw some people.**
- **Tell a partner about it.**

- **Write about what happens.**

Word-bank

One day

Once

Once upon a time

Teachers' note The picture is incomplete to allow the children to draw their own ideas about what might happen in the setting. You could discuss castles the children have come across in stories. Who lived in them and what happened there? Make a word-bank of vocabulary in response to the children's ideas.

Developing Literacy
Text Level Year R
© A & C Black 2000

Biscuits

- **Write the words for the recipe.**

Mix _____

_____ .

Rub in _____

_____ .

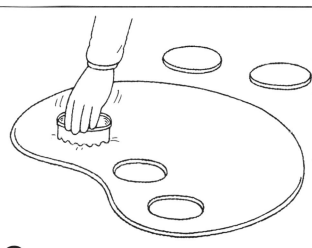
dough

Roll out _____

_____ .

Cut _____

_____ .

Now try this!

- **Draw and write the rest of the recipe.**

Word-bank

bake	baking tray
oven	put

Teachers' note Before the lesson, you could make biscuits with the children, letting them follow the recipe on this page. Before continuing beyond the part illustrated here, ask them what happens after the fourth picture. The recipe could also be cut up for the children to sequence before they complete it.

Developing Literacy
Text Level Year R
© A & C Black 2000

The cook's shopping list

The cook wants to make some biscuits.

- **Draw and write the cook's shopping list.**

- **Write a shopping list for the Three Bears.**

Teachers' note Page 57 should be completed first. Let the children re-read their biscuit recipe, and ask them to name all the ingredients. The ingredients could be set out so that the children can copy the words from their labels. The children could write shopping lists for other story characters.

**Developing Literacy
Text Level Year R
© A & C Black 2000**

Jack forgets to take things to school.

trainers

book

lunch box

- **Write notes for Jack's memory board.**

- **Draw three other things on Jack's memory board.**
- **Write a note for <u>your</u> memory board.**

Now try this!

Teachers' note Discuss the things which the children sometimes have to remember to bring to school. How do they make sure they don't forget? Show them a real memory board with notes pinned on to it and invite children to come out and read the notes.

Developing Literacy
Text Level Year R
© A & C Black 2000

Boat race

The children raced their boats.

• **Write about the boat race.**

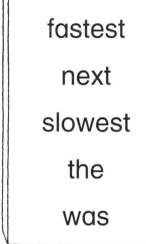

This boat was _____ .

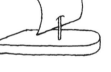

This boat _____ .

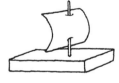

This _____ .

Word-bank

fastest

next

slowest

the

was

• **Write about this boat race.**

Now try this!

Teachers' note Ask the children to look at the picture and describe the way in which the boats were raced. Which one was the fastest? Which one was next and which was the slowest? How can they tell?

**Developing Literacy
Text Level Year R
© A & C Black 2000**

A letter to Humpty Dumpty

- **Write a letter to Humpty Dumpty in hospital.**

Dear Humpty Dumpty

- **What would you like to ask Humpty Dumpty?**
- **Write the question.**

Now try this!

Teachers' note Read the rhyme *Humpty Dumpty* as a shared text and ask the children what is going to happen to Humpty Dumpty. What could they write to make him feel better? Make a word-bank in response to their ideas. Suggest that they end their letters with a question so that Humpty Dumpty will reply. After the activity write a 'reply' to the class, from Humpty Dumpty.

Developing Literacy
Text Level Year R
© A & C Black 2000

Rhyme change

Pussy cat, pussy cat,
Where have you been?
I've been to London
To visit the Queen.

• **Change the rhyme. Draw a picture.**

Pussy cat, pussy cat,

What did you see?

I went to London

And saw a _____.

Pussy cat, pussy cat,

What will you do?

I'll go to London

And _____.

Now try this!

• **Write another rhyme which begins**
Pussy cat, pussy cat.

Teachers' note Read the rhyme with the children and ask them to say and point to the words which rhyme. Model some examples with them: for example, 'Pussy cat, pussy cat, what can you *see*? I can see a mouse behind a tree'.

Developing Literacy
Text Level Year R
© A & C Black 2000

Zoo poem

Off we went to the zoo today –
We saw a lion, and what did it say?

 Grr! Grr! Go away!

- **Write verses about these animals.**

Off we went to the zoo today –

We saw a _____, and what did it say?

 _____ _____ Go away!

Off we went to the zoo today –
We saw an _____, and what did it say?

_____ _____ Go away!

Now try this!

- **Write two other verses.**
- **Draw the pictures.**

Teachers' note Read the first verse with the children and ask them to say and point to the words which describe the sound made by the lion. Model some examples with them: for example, Off we went to the zoo today – We saw a monkey, and what did it say? 'Chatter! Chatter! Go away!'

Developing Literacy
Text Level Year R
© A & C Black 2000

Musical poem

• Write the sounds of the instruments.

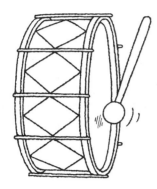

Boom boom
Goes the drum.

_____

Goes the triangle.

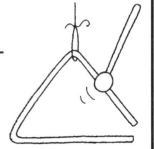

_____

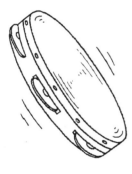

Goes the tambourine.

_____

Go the castanets.

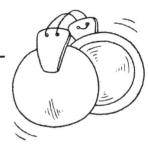

_____

Go the bells.

• Write the sound of another instrument.

• Draw the picture.

Now try this!

Teachers' note Begin by inviting the children to take turns to try an instrument; ask the others to make its sound and then to 'say' its sound; ask them to help you to write the sound, for example, 'chucka chucka,' go the maracas.

Developing Literacy
Text Level Year R
© A & C Black 2000